E. Moutsou - S. Parker

ELEMENTARY

listening
speaking
reading
writing

plus

publications

New Plus Elementary Listening-Speaking-Reading-Writing

E. Moutsou - S. Parker

Published by: **MM Publications**
www.mmpublications.com
info@mmpublications.com

Offices
UK China Cyprus Greece Korea Poland Turkey USA
Associated companies and representatives throughout the world.

Produced in the EU

ISBN: 978-960-379-967-2 C1905002015-16185

Introduction

Welcome to **Plus Elementary**. This book has been designed to help young learners of English at Elementary level develop their listening, speaking, reading and writing skills in an integrated way.

The book consists of ten units. Each unit is based on a different topic and is divided into six sections (Warm-up, Listening, Speaking, Pre-Writing, Reading and Writing), which are closely linked to each other. All units include a variety of tasks and activities which are necessary for the practice and consolidation of vocabulary, structures and various skills as well as a number of *Remember!* boxes, highlighting some important points. The last activity in the writing section is always a project, which the students can prepare and present on the special project pages provided at the end of the book.

Contents

unit 01

About myself

WARM-UP

1 Look at the words below and write them under the correct heading.

Maths

Science

hamster

monkey

parrot

ice skating

cycling

bungee jumping

rabbit

goldfish

Geography

History

table tennis

ballet

HOBBIES / SPORTS	PETS	SCHOOL SUBJECTS

2 **The pictures below show different sports and hobbies. Write the name of the sport or hobby under each picture. Then, in pairs, discuss which of them you like and why. Look at the Remember box and use the vocabulary given.**

Remember !

- **like**
  don't like
  enjoy
  am interested in } noun **+ or** -ing
- Use **because** to explain why.
- Use the **Present Simple** for habits, repeated actions or permanent states.

I **like** ice skat**ing because** I like winter sports.
I **don't like** ballet.
I **enjoy** play**ing** table tennis.
I **am interested in** mak**ing** jewellery.

VOCABULARY

boring	outdoors
dangerous	rollerblades
exciting	talent
exercise	team sport
fun	tiring
interesting	trendy
keep fit	

LISTENING

1 **Listen to three students talking about themselves. What is each of the students talking about? Tick (✓) the correct boxes. Look at the example.**

	STEFAN	CAROLINE	ROMEK
Age	✓		✓
Nationality			
Family			
Pet			
School			
Hobbies / Sports			

2 **Listen to the recording again and choose the best answer. Circle a, b or c.**

1 Stefan's sister likes a. b.  c. 

2 Stefan's pet is a a.   b. c. 

3 Caroline goes to school a.  b.  c. 

4 Caroline doesn't a.  b.  c. 

5 Romek lives in a a.  b. c. 

6 Romek's favourite subjects are a.  b. c. 

SPEAKING

1 **Work in pairs. Take turns to be Student A and Student B.**

Student A

You meet Student B for the first time. Ask Student B questions to find out more about him/her. Use the ideas given.

ideas!

how / old?
where / come from?
where / live?
have got / brothers or sisters?
have got / a pet?
what / hobbies?

Student B

Look at the map on the next page and imagine you are one of the four people. Introduce yourself to Student A and answer his/her questions. Begin: *Hello. I'm ...*

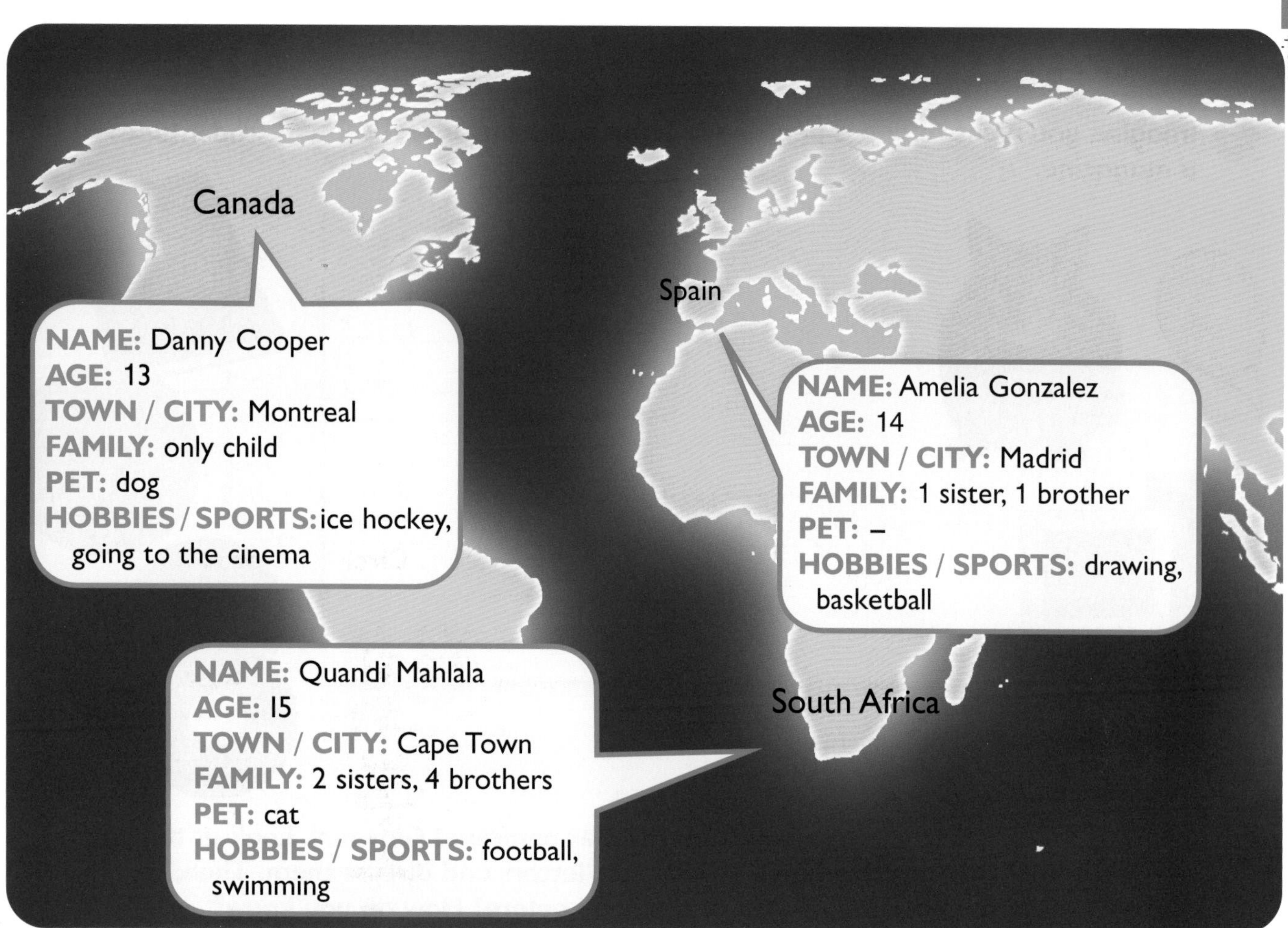

2 **Talk in pairs or small groups. Imagine that you want a penfriend. You have seen the following advertisements for penfriends in a magazine. Which of the people below do you want to have as a penfriend? Why?**

My name is Chang and I'm from Hong Kong. I'm 13 years old and I'm interested in computers. I am an only child, but I've got lots of friends.
Please write to: Chang Shik
54 Connaught Road
Hong Kong
China

My name is Maria Pereira and I'm 14 and a half years old. I live with my parents and baby brother in São Paulo. I love football and I also enjoy gymnastics.
Please write to: Maria Pereira
75 Ramalho Street
São Paulo
Brazil

My name is Vincent and I'm from the Netherlands. I'm eleven years old and I have an Alsatian dog. In my free time I like playing sports. My favourite hobby is collecting seashells.
Please write to: Vincent Van Damm
120 Langestraat
Amsterdam
The Netherlands

PRE-WRITING

Imagine you want to find a penfriend. Write a similar advertisement about yourself for a magazine.

READING

1 **Below is a letter that Ann-Marie has sent to her penfriend Giovanni. Look at the points which are in blue about the layout of informal letters and discuss them. Then, read Ann-Marie's letter. Has she written to Giovanni before? How do you know?**

Write your address.

137 Francis Way
Witham
Essex CM8 3QT
England

30 March 2005

Write the date below the address.

Begin with *Dear + first name.*

Put a comma after the name.

Dear Giovanni,

How are you? I'm happy we will be penfriends. Let me tell you about myself.

My name is Ann-Marie Lindsay and I am thirteen years old. I'm English and I live in a small town outside London. I've got a brother and a sister. My brother is three years younger than me and my sister is a baby. Have you got any brothers or sisters? I want to know all about you! Are you the outdoor type? I am! In my free time I enjoy cycling with my friends. My favourite sport is netball and I am the shooter for the school team. At school I really enjoy our English class because we write a lot of stories. I also like History, but I don't like Science. Have you got a favourite subject?

Well, that's all for now. I look forward to hearing from you.

Best wishes,
Ann-Marie

Start every paragraph under the comma. Always begin with a capital.

End your letter with 'Best wishes' or 'Bye for now'. Put a comma after it and write your first name under it.

2 **Now read Giovanni's letter to Ann-Marie and complete the chart below.**

500 Consalvo Street
Napoli 80126
Italy

27 April 2005

Dear Ann-Marie,

How are you? Thank you for your letter. It was a nice surprise. Let me tell you a few things about myself.

My name is Giovanni Benini, but my friends call me 'Baggio', like the footballer, Roberto Baggio. I'm thirteen and I'm from Italy. I've got two older brothers and a pet dog. I like outdoor activities, too. My favourite sport is football, of course, and I play for the school team. You say you like playing netball, but I don't know what netball is. Is it like basketball? School, in general, is a bit boring but I have fun with my friends. My favourite subject is English. You see, I want to learn the language well because I want to come to England one day.

Well, that's all about me. Write back soon.

Bye for now,
Giovanni

	ANN-MARIE	GIOVANNI
nationality		
brother(s)/sister(s)		
pet		
hobbies		
favourite subject(s)		

3 **Read the sentences below. Write T for True or F for False in the boxes.**

a. Ann-Marie is as old as Giovanni. ☐

b. Ann-Marie's sister is older than her. ☐

c. Giovanni has got a nickname. ☐

d. Ann-Marie lives in London. ☐

e. Giovanni doesn't like animals. ☐

f. Ann-Marie and Giovanni like sport. ☐

g. Ann-Marie likes all school subjects. ☐

h. Giovanni wants to travel abroad. ☐

i. Ann-Marie and Giovanni like English for the same reason. ☐

WRITING

1 Match A and B and complete the blanks with and or but to make sentences. Look at the example and the Remember box below.

A	B
My name's Yuki	______ I haven't got any brothers.
I have got two older sisters, Satoko and May,	______ I play the samisen, a Japanese instrument.
I'm very interested in music	______ I usually play it with my friend Honda.
I also enjoy indoor activities like reading	______ I like playing computer games.
My favourite sport is table tennis	and I live in Osaka.
Honda lives next door	______ I don't really like outdoor sports.
My favourite subject is Computer Science	______ we walk to school together every day.

Remember!

Use:
- **and** to join similar ideas (words/sentences)
- **but** to join two opposite ideas.

2 Form questions using the words given.

a. you / like / music?

____

b. what / be / your favourite sport?

____

c. you / collect / stamps or coins?

____

d. you / have got / a pet?

____

e. what / you / do / in your free time?

____

f. what / be / your favourite school subject?

____

3 **Imagine that you are Fernando. Look at the pictures and write sentences about yourself, as in the example. Use the verbs given.**

(have got)

e.g. *I have got a baby sister and two older brothers.*

(come)

a. ____________________

(be)

b. ____________________

(go)

c. ____________________

(have got)

d. ____________________

(enjoy)

e. ____________________

Remember!

When you are writing a letter to a penfriend for the first time, you should write three paragraphs.

- In the second paragraph, introduce yourself and then write about some of the following:

age
nationality
town/city where you live
family
pet
school/subjects
hobbies/sports

- Don't forget to ask your new penfriend questions.
- Don't write very short sentences. Use **and** and **but**.

PROJECT

Look at the advertisements on page 9 again and choose a penfriend. Turn to page 77 and complete the letter to your new penfriend. In the space provided, stick a photo of yourself.

unit 02

My town

WARM-UP

1 **Look at the pictures below and the adjectives in the box. Which adjectives describe each place? Write them in the space under each picture. Then, make sentences about both places. Look at the Remember box.**

VOCABULARY

boring	lively	quiet
busy	modern	traditional
crowded	noisy	
healthy	polluted	

______________________________ ______________________________

______________________________ ______________________________

______________________________ ______________________________

______________________________ ______________________________

______________________________ ______________________________

Remember!

- Use **adjectives** when you are describing a place.

A town is a **quiet** place.

2 **Look at the map below. Which place on the map does each word describe? Write the number in the box next to each word.**

airport ☐ lake ☐ port ☐ railway station ☐ bridge ☐ museum ☐ castle ☐ river ☐ park ☐ motorway ☐ suburb ☐ city centre ☐ cathedral ☐

LISTENING

1 **Listen to a telephone conversation between two friends. Tick (✓) where Lorraine wants to go while in Glasgow.**

A Museum ☐ B Botanic gardens ☐ C Library ☐

D Department stores ☐ E Cinema ☐ F Theatre ☐

2 **Listen to the conversation again. Write T for True or F for False.**

a. Susan and Lorraine talk often on the phone. ☐
b. Susan used to live in Braintree. ☐
c. Braintree is a noisy town. ☐
d. Susan went to a museum with her parents. ☐
e. The biggest library in Europe is in Glasgow. ☐
f. There's nothing to do in Susan's neighbourhood. ☐
g. Lorraine is coming to Glasgow for Christmas. ☐

SPEAKING

1 **Work in pairs. Student A, read the fact file on Mexico below and Student B, read the fact file on the next page. Don't look at each other's information. Both fact files are the same, but different details are missing from them. Take turns to ask each other questions to find the missing details.**

Student A

MEXICO

Capital:	Mexico City
Population:	about **1** ____________
Language:	**2** ____________
Traditional dish:	Tortillas
Longest river:	The Rio Grande
Highest mountain:	Pico Orizaba
Famous sights:	The Pyramid of the Sun in Teotihuacan (City of the Gods), Uxmal (**3** ____________ Mayan ____________)

Student B

MEXICO

Capital: Mexico City
Population: about 104 million
Language: Spanish
Traditional dish: 1 ____________
Longest river: 2 ________________
Highest mountain: Pico Orizaba
Famous sights: 3 ________________ in Teotihuacan (City of the Gods), Uxmal (ancient Mayan city)

2 **Work in groups. Read what the children say about their town/city and take turns to say something similar about your town/city.**

My town is beautiful because it has got many historical buildings and lovely parks. The only problem is that there are no interesting places for young people to go to.

I love my city because there are so many places to go to, like theatres and cinemas. I also like the modern sports centres.

PRE-WRITING

Use the information in the chart below to write a few sentences about Rome.

____
____
____
____

CITY CHART

CITY: Rome
LOCATION: central Italy
GEOGRAPHICAL FEATURE: on the River Tiber
POPULATION: 3 million
FAMOUS SIGHTS: the Colosseum, the Pantheon, St Peter's Basilica, the Vatican

____
____
____
____
____
____

READING

1 Read the description of Amsterdam below. Then look at pictures A, B and C. Can you guess which one is Amsterdam?

I live in Amsterdam, the capital of the Netherlands. Amsterdam is different from any other city in the world because it is below sea level. There are lots of canals in the city which divide it into islands. That's why there are four hundred bridges in the city. Amsterdam also has many interesting sights. The most important ones are two churches which are over five hundred years old and a seventeenth century palace. There are also lots of famous museums full of classical and modern paintings.

Amsterdam is a beautiful city and I like it very much. The land is flat and low, so it's the perfect place for cycling. There are many bicycle lanes and I go cycling with my friends every day. Many tourists also visit my city. I feel very lucky, because I get the chance to meet people from all over the world.

A

B

C

2 Read the sentences below. Write T for True or F for False in the boxes.

a. The bridges in Amsterdam join the islands. ☐

b. The palace in Amsterdam is older than the churches. ☐

c. There aren't any hills in Amsterdam. ☐

d. The writer likes riding his bicycle. ☐

e. The writer enjoys meeting people from abroad. ☐

WRITING

1 Join the two sentences using which, as in the example. Look at the Remember box.

e.g. The Arc de Triomphe is a monument. It stands in the centre of Paris.
The Arc de Triomphe is a monument which stands in the centre of Paris.

a. At the top of the hill there is a church. The church is one hundred years old.

____

____

b. I live in a town. It has got a population of 200,000 people.

____

____

c. In Cairo there are many historical buildings. They are in the old part of the city.

____

____

d. In my town there is a river. The river runs through the town centre.

____

____

e. On the west side there is a bridge. It connects the city centre with the suburbs.

____

____

Remember!

- When you are describing a place, don't write very short sentences and don't repeat the same words all the time.
- Use **which** to replace **things**.

I live in a city. ~~It~~ **which** has got a population of six million people.

2 Look at the pictures below and on the next page. Do you like these places? Why/Why not? Write a sentence about each place as in the example.

Sorrento, Italy

Isle of Lewis, Scotland

New York, USA

e.g. I like Sorrento because I like living by the sea.

a. ______________________________

b. ______________________________

Ottawa, Canada

c. ______________________

____

Hong Kong, China

d. ______________________

____

Las Vegas, USA

e. ______________________

____

3 Complete the chart below about your city/town.

CITY / TOWN CHART

CITY / TOWN: ______________________

LOCATION: ______________________

GEOGRAPHICAL FEATURE(S): ______________________

____

POPULATION: ______________________

FAMOUS SIGHT(S): ______________________

____

Remember !

When you are describing a city/town, you should write two paragraphs.

- In the first paragraph, write information about the city/town like:

  name
  location
  geographical features
  population
  famous sights

- In the second paragraph, write if you like or don't like this city/town. Explain why.

PROJECT

Turn to page 79 and write a description of your city/town. Use the information from the City/Town Chart you completed in WRITING 3. In the space provided, stick photos or draw pictures of your city/town.

unit 03

This is what happened

WARM-UP

1 **Work in pairs. Take turns to interview each other. Choose a question from box A.**

A **Have you ever** had an accident? / lost your wallet? / seen a wild animal? / found something valuable? / broken an arm or a leg?

Your partner answers **NO** → Choose another question from box **A**.

Your partner answers **YES** → Continue with the questions in box **B**.

B When did it happen?
Where did it happen?
Who was with you?

2 **Read the situations below and complete the sentences. Use the adjectives in the box.**

excited	shocked	surprised	scared	embarrassed

Lots of different things happened to me last week. This is how I felt ...

e.g. At the weekend I went camping. When I saw a snake, I was scared/shocked .

a. On Monday it was my birthday. When I arrived home, I was ____________ .

b. On Tuesday I went to school wearing my slippers. When I realised it, I felt ____________ .

c. On Wednesday my dog tore up all my books. When I saw the mess in my room, I was ____________ .

d. On Thursday I saw the list for the basketball team. When I saw my name on the noticeboard, I got ____________ .

LISTENING

1 **Listen to a boy describing an experience he had. Look at the pictures A-F below and tick (✓) the three which show what happened.**

A

B

C

D

E

F

2 **Listen to the recording again. Complete the clocks in the sentences below with the correct times. Look at the example.**

e.g. The game began at 

b. The second half began at 

a. The fight happened at 

c. The game finished at 

SPEAKING

1 **a. Work in pairs. Put the pictures A-E below in the correct order to show what happened to the two boys. Write the numbers 1-5 in the boxes.**

b. Work in pairs. Describe what happened in the pictures above to your class but change one or two details. One of you should describe what happened in pictures A, B and C and the other should describe what happened in pictures D and E. The class must find the changes you have made. Use the vocabulary and the expressions given. Look at the Remember box on the next page.

VOCABULARY

Hallowe'en	arrive	scream
dress up	ring	police car
burglar	doorbell	explain
wear	no answer	catch
clothes	look	bring
gloves	through	take off
balaclava	window	grandsons
decide	real	

EXPRESSIONS

Last year, on ...
When they arrived ... but ...
As they were ...
She thought that they ...
Immediately, ...
In the end, ...
She couldn't believe her eyes!
They were ...

Remember!

When you are describing something that happened in the past, use the Past Simple and the Past Progressive.

- Use the **Past Simple** for completed actions which happened one after the other.
- Use the **Past Progressive** for longer actions which were interrupted by shorter ones, or for two actions which were happening at the same time.

When I **finished** my homework, I **went** out with my friends.
As I **was watching** TV, I **heard** a strange noise.
While I **was walking** in the woods, I **was listening** to my personal stereo.

2 **Work in pairs. Choose one of the situations A or B below and imagine you are the person in the picture. Take turns to describe what happened to you and what you did afterwards. You can use the vocabulary and the expressions given.**

A

Start like this: One day I was eating a sandwich on my way home from school.

VOCABULARY

start	stop
chase	tired
afraid	realise
run	hungry
decide	give

EXPRESSIONS

Suddenly, ...
I was ..., so ...
A few minutes later ... because ...
Then, ...
In the end, ...

B

Start like this: One day I went to the hairdresser's because I wanted to dye my hair blonde.

VOCABULARY

finish	pink
look	see
myself	scream
mirror	black

EXPRESSIONS

When ...
I was ... because ...
As soon as ...
In the end, ...

3 **Read the diary page below. Then tell the rest of the class about something that happened to you. You can describe something funny, surprising, unpleasant or embarrassing.**

Tuesday, 20th November
Today was the best day of my life! I found a beautiful puppy near my house and I took him home. Mum was delighted and let me keep him. Oh, I'm so happy! I'll call him Spotty because he's got black spots on his back.

PRE-WRITING

Complete the diary below. Write a few sentences about something that happened to you.

READING

1 **Read the text on the next page. Five sentences are missing. Complete blanks 1-5 with the sentences A-E below.**

A We waited for some time but the coach didn't return.

B We left early in the morning because it was a two-hour journey.

C All our classmates were waving at us.

D Just as I was dialling my home number, I looked up and couldn't believe my eyes!

E While we were waiting, my friend and I went to the shop to buy some snacks.

Last Wednesday my class went on a trip to London Zoo. It was our first school excursion and we were all very excited.

__________ (1) Halfway to the zoo we stopped at a service station because the driver of the coach wanted to check something. __________ (2) We soon forgot about the time. I was at the cash desk when I suddenly saw our coach leaving without us! My friend and I ran outside and started shouting, but it was no good. __________ (3) Fifteen minutes later I decided to call my parents.

__________ (4) Our coach was driving into the car park. __________ (5) We were so relieved!

When we got back on the coach, our teacher was very angry. Fortunately, she was also glad to see us and did not punish us. However, we promised to be more careful in the future.

2 Choose the best title for this text. Why are the other two titles not appropriate?

A The day I got lost

B A trip with a bad start

C A visit to London Zoo

WRITING

1 Read the two texts below. Complete the sentences with the Past Simple or the Past Progressive of the verbs in brackets. Look at the examples.

a. One day, as my brother and I __were cycling__ (cycle) along a country road, we __saw__ (see) a small path. We **(1)** __________ (get) off our bikes and **(2)** __________ (follow) the path on foot. About an hour later, we **(3)** __________ (get) tired and **(4)** __________ (stop) to rest. We **(5)** __________ (have) a snack when we **(6)** __________ (hear) a strange noise behind us in the bushes. We **(7)** __________ (be) terrified. We **(8)** __________ (jump) up and **(9)** __________ (leave) immediately, because we **(10)** __________ (not want) to meet any wild animals.

b. One day while I **(1)** __________ (walk) on the beach, I **(2)** __________ (find) a gold identity bracelet. It was very beautiful. I **(3)** __________ (know) it was worth a lot, but I **(4)** __________ (not know) what to do with it. When I **(5)** __________ (look) at it more closely, I **(6)** __________ (notice) the name *MARY* written on it. Then I **(7)** __________ (start) shouting *Mary*. A few minutes later I **(8)** __________ (see) a woman in the distance. As she **(9)** __________ (come) nearer, I could see that she **(10)** __________ (smile) at me. Obviously, the bracelet was hers.

2 Join the pairs of sentences using the linking words/phrases in brackets, as in the example. Look at the Remember box below.

e.g. I was waiting for the bus. Two men in masks jumped out of a car and ran into the bank. (while)
While I was waiting for the bus, two men in masks jumped out of a car and ran into the bank.

a. I saw the fire in my kitchen. I called the fire brigade. (as soon as)

____

____

b. I entered my house. I saw that the TV set was missing. (when)

____

____

c. We were driving to our country house. My brother and I were singing and laughing. (while)

____

____

d. We were walking in the woods. A bear suddenly appeared in front of us. (as)

____

____

e. I heard strange noises in the middle of the night. I called the police. (so)

____

____

f. Yesterday my friends and I went for a walk in the city. We got lost. (but)

____

____

Remember!

- When you are describing events, don't write very short sentences. Use **linking words/phrases** to join them. You can use some of the linking words/phrases below.

when	so
while	but
as	because
as soon as	

3 **Look at SPEAKING 2 on page 23 again. Choose one of the situations A or B and write a few sentences about it. Use linking words/phrases.**

____
____
____
____
____
____

4 **Think of something funny that has happened to you. Answer the questions below in note form.**

When did it happen? ______________________________

Where did it happen? ______________________________

Who was with you? ______________________________

What were you doing? ______________________________

What happened? 1. ______________________________

2. ______________________________

3. ______________________________

4. ______________________________, etc.

How did you feel? ______________________________

What happened in the end? ______________________________

Remember !

- When you are writing about something that has happened to you, you should write three paragraphs. In these paragraphs you can describe the event by answering the questions in WRITING 4.
- Describe the events in the order in which they happened. Use the Past Simple and the Past Progressive as well as linking words/phrases.
- Use adjectives to describe how you felt.

PROJECT

Turn to page 81 and write about something funny that has happened to you. Use the notes you made in WRITING 4. In the space provided, draw pictures about your experience.

04 unit

My holidays

WARM-UP

1 **Below are some activities that people do while they are on holiday. Put them under the correct heading. Some activities can go under more than one heading.**

sunbathing | exploring nature | visiting museums | tasting local food | shopping

windsurfing | hiking | fishing | staying at hotels | meeting local people | camping

Holiday by the sea	Holiday in the mountains	Touring holiday in a city

2 **Complete the crossword with adjectives which describe the weather.**

LISTENING

1 **Listen to the recording. Two people who are on holiday in Finland are having a conversation in a café. What are they talking about? Circle a, b or c.**

a. Things they have already done together.
b. Their plans for the rest of the holiday.
c. Different things each of them has done.

2 **Listen to the recording again and look at pictures A-F below. Who did each activity? Write M for Mark or K for Karen in the boxes.**

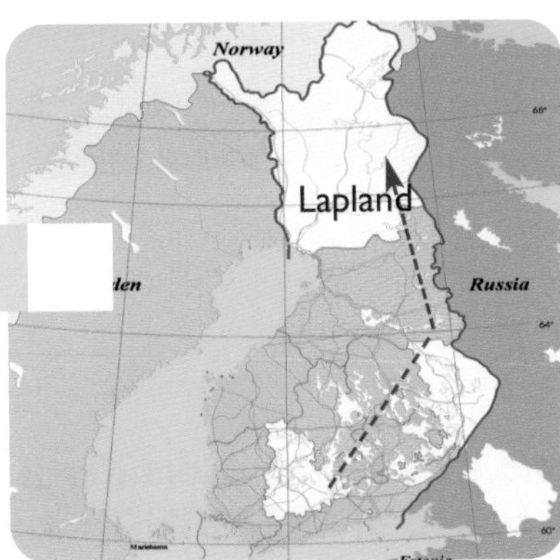

SPEAKING

1 **Work in groups of four. What is the best holiday you have ever had? Look at the questions and write your answers on the chart. Then, take turns to interview the other students in your group and complete the chart.**

	YOU	STUDENT 1	STUDENT 2	STUDENT 3
Where did you go?				
Who did you go with?				
How long did you stay there?				
What did you do there?				
Why did you like it?				

When you have finished, present the results of your survey to the class.

e.g. *All of us went on holiday with our parents. Two of us / Two students in my group went to an island.*

2 **Work in groups of three or four. Imagine that you are on holiday at one of the places A-D below, but don't tell the others in your group. Describe what you are doing at the moment and later on in the day. The rest of the group must guess where you are. Look at the Remember box below.**

e.g. *At the moment I'm snorkelling with my friends. Tonight I'm going to a restaurant.*
So, you are in...

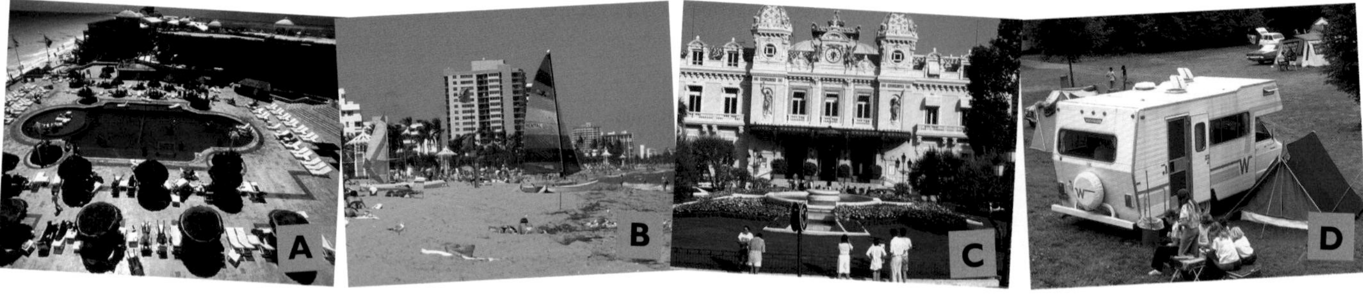

PRE-WRITING

Read the postcard below and guess where Jennifer is. Then imagine that you're on holiday in the place you discussed in SPEAKING 1 and write a similar postcard to a friend. Look at the Remember box.

Dear Stuart,
I love it here, but it's so cold! Even the horses wear furry hats! Yesterday, Tim and I visited some museums and a cathedral. I have taken lots of pictures of churches, monuments and Red Square. Tomorrow, we're going to a performance of the Bolshoi Ballet.

See you soon,
Jennifer

Stuart Bc
137 Gras
Lancaste
Lancash
Englanc

Dear ________,
It's great here in ________
Yesterday, ________
____
I have ________
____
Tomorrow, ________
____

See you soon,
____

Remember!

Use the **Present Progressive:**
- for actions which are happening at the moment of speaking.
- for actions which you have planned to do in the near future.

My brother **is swimming** now.
I'm visiting a museum this afternoon.

Use the **Present Perfect Simple:**
- for actions which happened in the past but we don't say when exactly.
- for actions which started in the past and continue up to the present.

I **have visited** two museums.
I **have been** in Hungary for one week.

READING

1 **Look at the boxes a-d below. Where should this information go in the letter? Write your answers on the letter.**

a. Ngorongoro C.A.
Tanzania
Africa

b. Love,
Jill

c. Dear Meg,

d. Thursday, June 20th

How are you? My parents and I have left Kenya and are now in Tanzania. We have been here for four days. We are having a great time! Let me tell you about it.

On Monday, we visited Lake Victoria, which is the largest lake in Africa. We wanted to go on a boat ride, but we couldn't because it was raining. So, we went to a restaurant and tasted the local food instead. It was delicious! I even tried fried bananas! The next day we arrived at the Serengeti National Park and went on a two-day safari in a jeep. It was so exciting! We saw elephants, zebras, giraffes and rhinos. I took lots of photos of them which I'll show you when I get back. Oh, and something else. Yesterday, when we were about to leave, I saw a snake. I was shocked! Anyway, today it was hot and sunny, so our guide took us to the Ngorongoro Conservation Area. We saw some flamingos there and then visited some archaeological sites. Tomorrow, we're travelling to Mount Kilimanjaro. We're also visiting some Masai villages. I can't wait!

Well, that's all my news for now. I hope to see you on Sunday when I get back.

2 **Read the letter above and complete the chart about Jill's holiday.**

DAY	PLACE	ACTIVITIES-EVENTS
Monday	(1)________	She went to a restaurant and (2)________.
Tuesday	(3)________	(4)________. She saw wild animals and (5)________.
Wednesday	(6)________	She continued the safari and (7)________.
Thursday	(8)________	She saw flamingos and (9)________.
Friday	Mount Kilimanjaro	(10)________.

3 **Read the letter again. What do the following words refer to?**

e.g. here (line 2): Tanzania

a. which (line 4): ______

b. It (line 7): ______

c. The next day (line 8): ______

d. It (line 9): ______

e. them (line 11): ______

f. us (line 14): ______

g. there (line 15): ______

WRITING

1 **Complete the blanks with the words in the box. Look at the example and the Remember box below.**

he	it	we	they	here	him	us	them	there

a. The nearest town to our hotel is five miles away. **The town →** It is beautiful and many tourists visit (**1**) **the town →** ______ in the summer. My parents and I go (**2**) **to the town →** ______ nearly every evening because (**3**) **my parents and I →** ______ love eating in the local restaurants. (**4**) **The restaurants →** ______ serve traditional Greek food, which is fantastic!

b. My cousin Ian and I are having a great time at the Blue Forest Camp. It was a bit difficult for (**1**) **Ian and me →** ______ in the beginning, but (**2**) **Ian and I →** ______ are organised now. So, (**3**) **Ian and I →** ______ are planning to stay (**4**) **at the Blue Forest Camp →** ______ longer. Yesterday morning Ian went fishing at a nearby lake but I didn't go with (**5**) **Ian →** ______ because I was tired. (**6**) **Ian →** ______ caught three big fish and (**7**) **Ian and I →** ______ ate (**8**) **the fish →** ______ for lunch. (**9**) **The fish →** ______ were absolutely delicious!

Remember!

- Don't repeat the same words all the time. Instead, use words like:

he / she / it / we / they
him / her / it / us / them
here / there

2 **a. Emily has written a letter to her friend Ronald. Read the first paragraph below and complete the blanks 1-5 with the missing words.**

December, 27th

Dear Ronald,

Hi! I ______ (**1**) you are fine. I am on ______ (**2**) in Switzerland with my parents and my brother. I'm ______ (**3**) to tell you all ______ (**4**) it. I'm having a great ______ (**5**)!

b. Now look at the pictures and the notes below and complete the next part of Emily's letter to Ronald.

I / sit / in outdoor café

I / have / cup / hot chocolate

my brother and I / take / a cable car / to top of mountain

we / go / cross-country skiing

I / also / go / ice skating

we / go / to / Geneva

we / want / tour / city

we / also / visit / Lake Geneva

The weather has been fantastic so far! It's sunny today and at the moment ______________________ (**1**). ______________________ (**2**). Yesterday, ______________________ (**3**). The view was so beautiful from up there! ______________________ (**4**) and it was fantastic! Have you tried it? ______________________ (**5**). I fell down lots of times, but I had fun. I want to do it again. Tomorrow, ______________ (**6**) for two days. ______________________(**7**). ______________________ (**8**).

c. Now read paragraphs A-C below. Which one is most suitable to end Emily's letter with? Why?

A Well, that's all about me for now. I hope you write back soon. Don't forget to send me a photo of yourself.
Bye for now,
Emily

B Well, I must go now because it's time for lunch. See you next week when I get back.
Your friend,
Emily

C Well, that's all for now. Write back soon and tell me what time your train arrives. I really want to see you again!
Love,
Emily

3 Imagine you are on holiday. Answer the questions below in note form.

Where are you? ______

How long have you been on holiday? ______

Who are you with? ______

Are you having a good time? ______

What is the weather like? ______

Which sights have you visited? ______

______

When did you visit them? ______

Have you done any activities/sport? What? ______

______

Are you doing anything interesting at the moment? ______

What are you doing tomorrow? ______

When are you going back home? ______

Remember!

When you are writing a letter while you are on holiday, you should write three paragraphs. In these paragraphs you can describe your holiday by answering the questions in WRITING 3.

- Start your letter with *Dear*.
  e.g. *Dear John,* *Dear Mum,*
- In the first paragraph, use a set phrase.
  e.g. *How are you?*
  I hope you are fine.
  Hello! I'm writing to tell you about my holiday.
- In the second paragraph, write what you have done/did/are doing now and what you are going to do in the future.
  Be careful with the tenses.
- In the third paragraph, use a set phrase.
  e.g. *Well, that's all for now.*
  See you soon!
  I must go now.
  See you when I get back.
- End your letter with a set word/phrase. Write your first name under this.
  e.g. *Yours,*
  Your friend,
  Love,
  Bye for now,
- Follow the layout for informal letters (page 10).

PROJECT

Turn to page 83 and write a letter to a friend or to your family describing your holiday. Use the notes you made in WRITING 3.

Superstars!

WARM-UP

1 **Look at the two letter grids below. In the first one, find ten words related to film stars. In the second one, find ten words related to pop stars.**

B	A	C	T	R	E	S	S	I	P
C	U	T	I	J	A	R	O	L	E
A	D	R	E	N	G	E	S	A	R
N	I	I	T	K	E	X	E	C	F
A	E	F	R	Q	U	M	P	T	O
W	N	S	U	E	Z	O	A	I	R
A	C	T	O	R	C	H	E	N	M
R	E	D	L	I	K	T	H	G	S
D	O	M	O	V	I	E	O	V	I
S	A	Y	V	T	H	E	A	R	E

C	H	I	N	G	A	P	S	L	O
S	I	N	G	E	R	Y	W	Y	U
I	T	S	O	M	V	I	E	R	T
C	H	T	C	B	A	N	R	I	T
A	N	R	S	O	N	G	E	C	F
L	F	U	L	E	N	U	Y	S	A
B	E	M	U	S	I	C	I	A	N
U	A	E	K	T	R	A	E	J	S
M	D	N	I	S	O	N	E	R	O
P	E	T	D	M	E	T	R	O	T

2 **Look at the pictures below and complete the descriptions. Use the adjectives in the box.**

handsome slim short beautiful big curly blonde

Nicole Kidman is pretty. She is _________ (**1**) and has got long _________ (**2**) hair.

Ethan Hawke is tall and _________ (**3**). He has got _________ (**4**) brown hair.

Beyoncé is a _________ (**5**) woman. She's got long _________(**6**) hair and _________ (**7**) brown eyes.

Remember!

For two or more **adjectives** before a noun, follow this order:

1. size / length	**2.** shape / type	**3.** colour	
big, small long, short	round, oval curly, straight, wavy	brown, green, black, blond(e)	+ noun

He has got **small green** eyes.
She has got **short wavy** hair.

LISTENING

1 Listen to part of a radio programme. The presenter is interviewing a rock singer's manager about the rock singer's career. Look at pictures A-E below and put the events in the correct order. Write the numbers 1-5 in the boxes. The first one has been done for you.

started a solo career

A

went on a US tour

B

started writing songs

C 1

played in a film

D

formed a band

E

2 Listen to the recording again and choose the best answer a, b or c.

1 How old was Mathew when he formed *The Dreamboys*?
a. 15
b. 17
c. 22

2 Mathew left the band because
a. it wasn't successful.
b. he became rich and famous.
c. he wanted to try something different.

3 Mathew's manager was worried about Mathew's career in the cinema because
a. Mathew gets bored easily.
b. he wasn't sure if Mathew could act.
c. Mathew's fans don't like surprises.

4 Will Mathew continue in the film business?
a. Yes
b. No
c. We do not know.

SPEAKING

1 **Work in pairs. Take turns to choose one of the six famous people below and describe his/her physical appearance without telling your partner who it is. Your partner has to guess which person you are describing. Look at the example.**

e.g. *This person has got long, straight hair ...* *So, it's ...*

Jennifer Lopez (singer, actress)

Justin Timberlake (singer)

Jim Carrey (actor)

Halle Berry (actress)

Robbie Williams (singer)

Tobey Maguire (actor)

2 **Work in pairs. Decide which of you is going to be Student A and which Student B. Student A should read the instructions below and Student B should read the instructions on the next page.**

STUDENT A

Look at the chart below and ask Student B questions in order to complete the missing information about Halle Berry.

Name: Halle Berry

Born: ____________

Where: ____________

Occupations: ____________

____

Successful films: ____________

____

Awards: ____________

Now, read the information about Jennifer Lopez on the Internet page below and answer Student B's questions.

File Edit View Favorites Tools Help

Back Forward Stop Refresh Home Search Favorites History Print

Address www.Jennifer Lopez.com

Jennifer Lopez

Nickname: J-Lo, La Lopez
Born: 24 July 1969
Where: Bronx, New York, USA
Occupations: singer, dancer, actress
Successful albums: *On the 6, J-Lo, This is me ... Then*
Successful films: *Selena, The Cell, Shall we Dance?*

Done

STUDENT B

Read the information about Halle Berry on the Internet page below and answer Student A's questions.

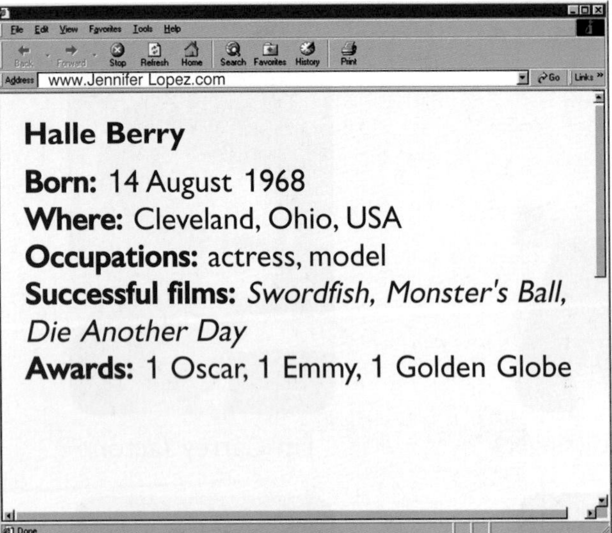

Halle Berry
Born: 14 August 1968
Where: Cleveland, Ohio, USA
Occupations: actress, model
Successful films: *Swordfish, Monster's Ball, Die Another Day*
Awards: 1 Oscar, 1 Emmy, 1 Golden Globe

Now, look at the chart below and ask Student A questions in order to complete the missing information about Jennifer Lopez.

Name: Jennifer Lopez
Nickname: ______________
Born: ______________
Where: ______________
Occupations: ______________
____
Successful albums: ______________
____
Successful films: ______________
____

PRE-WRITING

● **Below are two charts with information about famous people. Choose one person and write a few sentences about his/her career.**

Name:	Robbie Williams
Occupation:	singer
Successful albums:	*Life Thru a Lens, Angels, Swing When You Are Winning, Escapology*
Awards:	Best Male Solo Artist in Britain 1999, 2001, 2002, 2003, *Angels* best song of the past 25 years at BRIT Awards

Name:	Jim Carrey
Occupation:	actor, comedian
Successful films:	*The Mask, Liar Liar, The Truman Show, Man on the Moon*
Awards:	Golden Globe for performance in *The Truman Show*, nine MTV movie awards

____
____
____
____
____
____
____
____

READING

1 **Read the text below about a famous person.**

My favourite actor is Leonardo DiCaprio. He is the actor who played Jack Dawson in the film *Titanic*. The film was a blockbuster and Leonardo became famous all over the world. Leonardo has also starred in other successful films like: *The Beach*, *Gangs of New York* and *The Aviator*.

I really like Leonardo DiCaprio because he is a very talented actor who can play different roles. I also think he is very handsome. He has got blond hair and beautiful blue eyes. I believe Leonardo has got a great future ahead of him.

Find words in the text which mean:

a. very successful film ______________________
b. well-known ______________________
c. play in a film ______________________
d. good at something ______________________
e. good-looking ______________________

2 **Read the text again. Which of the following does the writer mention? Tick (✓) the correct boxes.**

a. Leonardo's plans for the future ☐
b. Leonardo's appearance ☐
c. facts about Leonardo's personal life ☐
d. films which Leonardo has played in ☐
e. his/her opinion about Leonardo ☐
f. facts about Leonardo's education ☐
g. Leonardo's opinion about the films he has played in ☐

WRITING

1 Join the two sentences using who or which as in the example. Look at the Remember box.

e.g. Tom Hanks is a very successful actor. He has won two Academy Awards.
Tom Hanks is a very successful actor who has won two Academy Awards.

a. In the film *My Left Foot*, Daniel Day-Lewis played a disabled man. That disabled man became a successful painter.

b. *Pretty Woman* was a very successful film. This film made Julia Roberts famous.

c. U2 are famous for their concerts. Their concerts include many special effects.

d. Angelina Jolie is an actress. She has starred in the film *Lara Croft Tomb Rider.*

e. Celine Dion is a talented singer. Celine Dion sings in both French and English.

- Don't write very short sentences and don't repeat the same words all the time.
- Use **who** to refer to **people** and **which** to refer to **things.**

Leonardo DiCaprio starred in *Romeo and Juliet.* ~~This film~~ which is a modern version of Shakespeare's play.

2 Think of two film stars and two pop stars you like. Why do you like them? Write four sentences in the bubbles on the next page. Use the prompts below. Look at the Remember box under the bubbles.

like
admire
be fond of

because

believe
think

that

act very well
perform beautifully on stage
have got a great voice
be very talented
style/music is original
can play different roles
the lyrics of his/her songs are beautiful
can play the guitar and the piano
can dance as well as act

____
____

____
____

____
____

____
____

Remember !

like
admire } + noun **or** him/her/them + because ...
be fond of

believe
think } + (that) ...

I **admire** his style.
I **am very fond of** her because she is talented.
I **believe** that they will be very successful in the future.

3 Who is your favourite film star or pop star? Complete one of the charts below.

Name of film star: ______________________
Successful films: ______________________
____
Other films: ______________________
____
Awards: ______________________
Special characteristics: ______________________
____
Appearance: ______________________
____
Future plans: ______________________

Name of pop star: ______________________
Name of band: ______________________
Successful albums: ______________________
____
Other albums: ______________________
____
Awards: ______________________
Special characteristics: ______________________
____
Appearance: ______________________
____
Future plans: ______________________

Remember !

When you are writing about your favourite superstar, write two paragraphs.

- Paragraph 1:
  - say who your favourite star is
  - write about his/her career and future plans
- Paragraph 2:
  - say why you like him/her
  - describe his/her appearance if necessary

PROJECT

Turn to page 85 and write about your favourite superstar. Use information from the chart you completed in WRITING 3. In the space provided, stick photos or draw pictures of your favourite superstar.

06 unit

In the future

WARM-UP

1 **Match the pictures with the words. Write the correct letter A-H in the box next to each word.**

planet ☐ dome ☐ pills ☐ robot ☐ space shuttle ☐ space station ☐

A

B

C

D

E

F

2 **What will life be like in the future? Complete the sentences below. Use will or won't and the verbs in the box.**

build do find need run disappear learn live

a. Children ______________ everything from computers so they ______________ to go to school.

b. People ______________ longer because doctors and scientists ______________ cures for many illnesses.

c. Robots ______________ the housework so people will have more free time.

d. Cars ______________ on petrol because there won't be any left.

e. People ______________ cities under the sea and perhaps on other planets.

f. Most plants and animals ______________ in the future because of pollution.

LISTENING

1 **Listen to three people talking about how things will change in the future. What is each speaker talking about? Choose from the words A-D and write your answers in the boxes below. You will not use one of the words.**

A food B computers C clothes D transport

Speaker 1 [ ] Speaker 2 [ ] Speaker 3 [ ]

2 **Listen to the recording again and read the sentences below. According to what the speakers say, write T for True or F for False in the boxes.**

a. In the future, people won't have to wash their clothes. [ ]

b. No one will cook in the future. [ ]

c. People won't drive cars in the future. [ ]

SPEAKING

1 **Work in small groups. Take turns to choose one of the three pictures A, B or C below, but don't tell the others in your group which one. Then, describe what cities, houses and transport will be like in one hundred years. Your group must guess which picture you are describing. Use the vocabulary and expressions on the next page and look at the Remember box.**

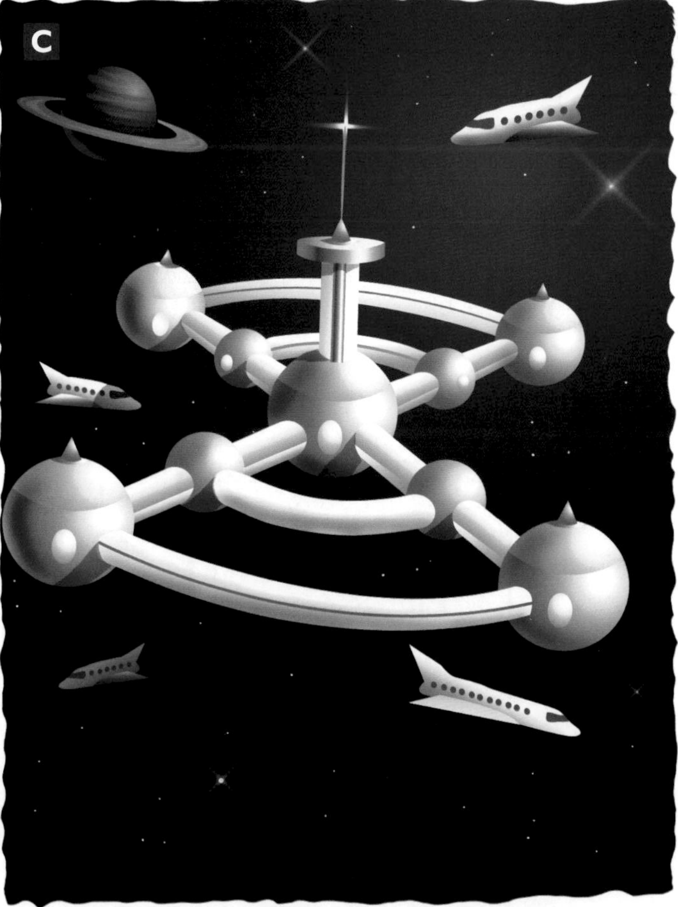

VOCABULARY

flat
automatic
building
motorway
submarine
traffic
travel
underground
underwater

EXPRESSIONS

I believe/think people will ...
In my opinion, ...
Everybody/People will probably ...
Perhaps ...
There will be no ...
We will certainly have ...
Also, ...
However, ...

Remember!

- Use the **Future *Will*** to predict the future.

I believe there **will be** more pollution in ten years' time.

2 **Work in pairs. Some of the pairs should predict what life at school will be like in the future while the other pairs should predict what life at home will be like. Then, each pair should report their ideas to the class. You can use the expressions above.**

PRE-WRITING

What do you think life at school or at home will be like in the future? Write a few sentences.

READING

1 **Read the text below about what life will be like in the future. What topics does the writer discuss?**

Life will be very different one hundred years from now. In my opinion, some things will be better and some things will be worse.

Firstly, people won't live on land. Our cities will be under the sea, in large domes. Special machines will provide oxygen and light, but the environment won't be the same. Trees and plants won't grow because there won't be any soil. As a result, people won't be able to grow their own food. Food will mainly be in the form of pills. If the sea isn't too polluted, people will also eat fish. What is more, I think people's everyday life will be different. They won't have to work long hours because computers and robots will help them. No one will have to do housework either. So, people will have more free time and they will be able to enjoy the things they like – sport, for example. Finally, I believe that people will be able to travel to the moon and to other planets for their holidays.

In conclusion, I think that life in the future won't be anything like it is now. Whatever happens, though, I'm sure the future will be interesting.

2 **Now look at the pictures below. Write a sentence about each of the pictures that is true according to the text. Begin with the words given and use will or won't.**

a. Robots ____________________

____

b. People ____________________

____

c. People ____________________

____

d. There ____________________

____

e. People ____________________

____

f. People ____________________

____

WRITING

1 Complete the conditional sentences below with your own ideas. Look at the example and the Remember box.

e.g. If cars use solar energy, there will be less pollution.

a. If robots do all the household chores, ______________________________
____

b. If we don't start protecting the environment, ______________________________
____

c. If scientists find cures to most illnesses, ______________________________
____

d. If scientists find life on another planet, ______________________________
____

e. If people do all their shopping by computer, ______________________________
____

f. If people continue to pollute rivers, ______________________________
____

Remember !

- Use **Conditional Sentences Type 1** for something which may happen in the future.
  If + Present Simple → Future *Will*

If students don't go to school in the future, they will have more free time.

2 Complete the sentences with will be able to, will have to or won't be able to. Look at the example.

e.g. In the near future computers will be able to understand spoken instructions.

a. In the year 2050 cars ________________ run on solar or electric power because there will be no petrol left.

b. By the year 2100 people ________________ grow any vegetables, as the land will be too polluted.

c. In the future most people ________________ work from home.

d. In the year 2200 people ________________ go on holiday to other galaxies.

3 **Read the text below and complete the blanks. Use the words/phrases in the box.**

what is more	finally	firstly	also	secondly

Homes in the future will be completely different from today's homes. They will have a central computer which will control different things around the house. ______________ (**1**), this computer will turn on the lights when someone enters the house. ______________ (**2**), it will know if there is a stranger in the house and, when there is, it will call the police immediately. It will ___________ (**3**) notify the fire brigade when there is a fire. ______________ (**4**), this computer will have a robot arm which will be able to play games, like chess, with people. ______________ (**5**), the computer will be able to understand spoken instructions and do some tasks.

Remember !

When you are writing a composition about what life will be like in the future, you should write three paragraphs.

- In the first paragraph, write your general opinion about the future.
- In the second paragraph, write your predictions about what life will be like and how it will change. You can write about some of the following:

homes	clothes
everyday life	computers/robots
work	technological advances
education	health
transport	the environment
food	space travel

Use words/phrases, like *firstly, secondly, what is more, also, finally,* to present your ideas.

- In the last paragraph, write your opinion again (but in different words) and make a general comment about the future. Begin with: *In conclusion.*

PROJECT

What do you think life will be like in one hundred year's time? Turn to page 87 and write a composition. In the space provided, draw pictures showing what life will be like in the future.

07 unit

A film I saw

WARM-UP

1 Look at the posters below and write what type of film each of them shows. Use the words in the box.

musical	animated film	love story	adventure film	comedy	horror film	science-fiction film

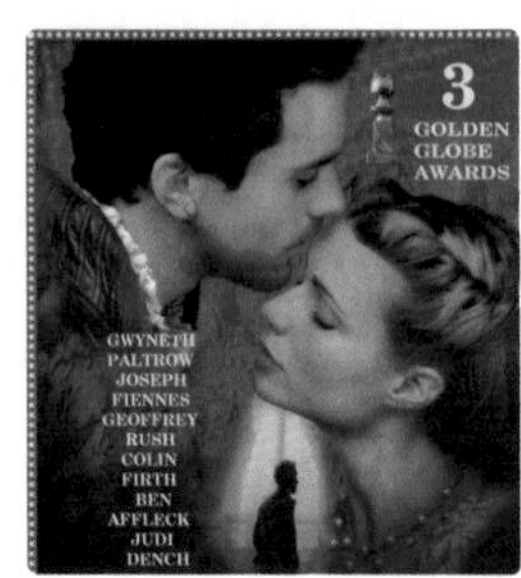

a. ________________ b. ________________ c. ________________ d. ________________

e. ________________ f. ________________ g. ________________

2 Complete the sentences and the crossword below. Look at the example.

ACROSS

3 Angelina Jolie is a popular ______________.

5 The final part of a film is called the ________________.

7 The music of a film is called the ______________.

8 Star Wars has amazing special ____________.

9 Tobey Maguire and Kirsten Dunst ____________ in Spiderman.

DOWN

1 The story of a film is called the ______________ .

2 The most important female or male part in the film is called the main ____________.

4 The clothes that actors wear in a film are called ________________.

6 Steven Spielberg is a famous ______________.

1 2
R
4
3 T
6
5 D
7 S U T
8 F S
9 S

3 **Read what the following people said about some of the films in activity 1 and circle the correct adjective. Look at the Remember box below.**

I really like the film *Star Wars*, as it has **amazed / amazing** special effects.

I was very **amused / amusing** by Eddie Murphy's acting in *Dr. Dolittle 2*.

Some scenes in the film *Scream* were very **frightened / frightening** and I had to keep my eyes closed.

Die Another Day is an action-packed film, full of suspense. I found it very **excited / exciting**.

I was very **moved / moving** by the story of *Shakespeare in Love* and I found the dialogues very **interested / interesting**.

- Use adjectives ending in **-ing** to describe **people** or **things**.
- Use adjectives ending in **-ed** to describe **people's feelings**.

The film was not **interesting** and I was **bored**.

LISTENING

1 **Listen to a radio presenter and a film critic discussing two films. Look at the film posters A-D below. Which two films are they discussing? Put a tick (✓) in the correct boxes.**

2 **Listen to the recording again and read the sentences below. In the boxes next to each sentence, write 1 if it is true for *Phone me Back*, 2 if it is true for *Monster Magic* and B if it is true for both films.**

a. The critic thinks this is a good film. ☐

b. The main characters in this film are a man and a woman. ☐

c. This film is funny. ☐

d. The physical appearance of the leading character changes in this film. ☐

e. The critic likes the acting in this film. ☐

f. The soundtrack of this film is great. ☐

g. The critic thinks this film has a very good plot. ☐

SPEAKING

1 **Play a game in two groups. Group A, choose a film that you have all seen, but don't tell Group B what it is. Each student, in turn, should say one sentence to describe the plot of the film. (Look at the Remember box below.) Group B, guess which film it is. Then, Group B, choose a film and continue the game.**

Remember !

- When you are describing the plot of a film, use the **Present Simple.**

The leading actor **wants** to find the lost boy, so he **goes** into the jungle to look for him.

2 **Work in pairs. Take turns to be Student A and Student B.**

Student A

You are a radio presenter and are interviewing Student B about a film he/she has seen. Ask him/her questions to find out what he/she liked or didn't like about the film. You can use the questions and the ideas below.

QUESTIONS

Which film have you seen recently?
What did you think of the ... of the film?
Did you like the ... ?
How did you find the ... ?
What did you like most about the film?

ideas!

plot
acting/actors
music
special effects

Student B

You are a film critic. Student A is interviewing you about a film you have seen. Think of a film you know well and answer Student A's questions. You can use the expressions and the vocabulary below.

EXPRESSIONS

I thought the ... was/were ...
In my opinion, the ...
I really liked the ...
I found the ...

VOCABULARY

clever	original
excellent	poor
exciting	(un)realistic
full of suspense	scary
interesting	wonderful

PRE-WRITING

In three or four sentences, write your opinion about a film you have seen. You can write about the plot, acting, costumes, music or special effects.

READING

1 Read the description of a film below. What is the topic of each paragraph?

Finding Neverland is a drama which is directed by Marc Forster. Johnny Depp and Kate Winslet star in this film. It is set in London in 1903 and is about the Scottish writer Sir James Matthew Barrie (Johnny Depp). The film tells the story of how Barrie gets the idea for his famous play *Peter Pan*. It all happens one day when Barrie meets Sylvia Llewelyn Davies (Kate Winslet) and her four sons in a park. Barrie's friendship with the Davies family inspires him to write a story about children who don't want to grow up.

I really enjoyed the film. The story is interesting and the acting is excellent. Johnny Depp and Kate Winslet give great performances. The four boys who play Sylvia's sons are also very good. *Finding Neverland* will make you feel like you are in a fairy tale. It is magical!

2 Read the text again and answer the questions below.

a. What type of film is *Finding Neverland*?

____

b. Who is the director?

____

c. Who are the main actors?

____

d. Where and when does the story of the film take place?

____

e. Who gives Sir James Matthew Barrie the idea for his play?

____

f. Which words/phrases in the second paragraph show that the writer liked the film?

____

WRITING

1 Read the description of the film below. Then complete the blanks with the Present Simple (Active or Passive) of the verbs in brackets. Look at the Remember box.

Shark's Tale is an animated comedy which **(1)** ____________ (set) in the world of saltwater fish. It's about Oscar - a little fish who **(2)** ____________ (tell) a big lie just to get fame, respect and love.

The son of Don Lino (a gangster shark boss) has an accident and **(3)** ____________ (die). Oscar **(4)** ____________ (find) at the scene. He **(5)** ____________ (pretend) that he killed the gangster's son in order to become famous. However, he soon **(6)** ____________ (find out) that he is playing a dangerous game in a world where small fish **(7)** ____________ (eat) by big fish.

Many famous actors give their voices to the characters. Don Lino **(8)** ____________ (play) by Robert de Niro and Will Smith **(9)** ____________ (have) the role of Oscar. *Shark's Tale* **(10)** ____________ (direct) by Bibo Bergeron and Vicky Jenson. It's really funny and the music is great!

Remember !

- We use the **Active Voice** to show **who** or **what** does something.
- We use the **Passive Voice** to show that something happens to the subject of the verb.

Johnny Depp **plays** the Scottish writer in *Finding Neverland*.
The Scottish writer in *Finding Neverland* **is played** by Johnny Depp.

2 Read the plot of the film below and write the missing sentences. Use the notes given.

Harry Potter and the Philosopher's Stone is an adventure film based on J.K. Rowling's novel of the same name. ____ **(1)**
His parents were killed in a car crash when he was still a baby. ____ **(2)**
He lives in a small room under the stairs. ____ **(3)**
On his eleventh birthday, Harry receives a mysterious letter from Hogwarts School of Witchcraft and Wizardry. He is chosen to become one of the students at that famous school of magic. ____ **(4)**
He is the son of a good wizard and witch who were killed by the evil Lord Valdemort. Valdemort also tried to kill Harry, but he couldn't. Before he disappeared, he left a mark on Harry's forehead.

At Hogwarts, Harry discovers that the world of magic is more interesting than the boring world he grew up in. ____ **(5)**
However, it's not all fun and games at Hogwarts. The evil Lord Valdemort is back!

(1) It / be / about / ten-year-old boy / call / Harry Potter / who / live / with / uncle / aunt /cousin
(2) Harry Potter / not have / easy / life
(3) Uncle Vernon / Aunt Petunia / not treat / him / very well / and / cousin Dudley / annoy / him / all the time
(4) Harry / also / learn / truth / about / himself
(5) He / meet / Ron Weasley / Hermione Granger / there / who / become / best / friends

3 Think of a film you have seen. Make notes about this film in the space below.

Name of film: ______________ Type of film: ______________

Actors: ______________ Director: ______________

Plot: ______________

____

Your opinion: ______________

	Excellent	Good	Bad	Why?
Plot	☐	☐	☐	______
Acting	☐	☐	☐	______
Music	☐	☐	☐	______
Special effects	☐	☐	☐	______
Ending	☐	☐	☐	______

Remember!

When you are writing a description of a film, you should write two paragraphs.

- In the first paragraph, write some general information about the film and the main points of the plot. Use the Present Simple and some of the phrases below.
- In the second paragraph, write your opinion, what you like or don't like about the film (e.g. *plot*, *acting*, *special effects*, *music*, *ending*). Use the Present Simple or Past Simple and some of the phrases below.

It's a comedy / an adventure film, etc.
... stars in this film.
... plays/has the main role.
The film is about ...
The hero/heroine of the film ...

I found the film exciting/boring.
This film is a blockbuster.
The film is full of suspense.
The story is interesting/boring.
The acting is excellent/bad.
The music is fantastic/awful.
The special effects are amazing/unrealistic.
The ending is surprising.

PROJECT

Turn to page 89 and write about a film you have seen recently. Use the notes you made in WRITING 3. In the space provided, stick or draw pictures that show scenes from the film.

unit 08

Would you like to come?

WARM-UP

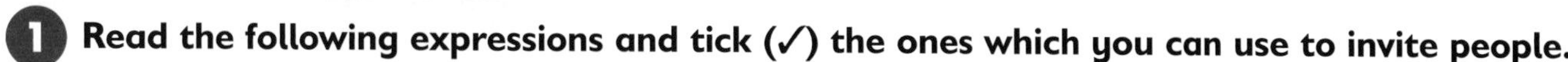

1 Read the following expressions and tick (✓) the ones which you can use to invite people.

a. I'm writing to invite you to ... ☐

b. Thanks for inviting me to ... ☐

c. How about coming to ...? ☐

d. I'm writing to thank you for the invitation ... ☐

e. I'd like to invite you to ... ☐

f. Would you like to come to ...? ☐

g. I'd love to come to... ☐

h. I'm writing to ask you to come to ... ☐

i. Can you make it to ...? ☐

2 The pictures a-f below show different types of parties. Unscramble the words under the pictures to find out what type of party each of them shows.

a. TDBIAYRH ____________________

b. NFAYC-SDESR ____________________

c. AUANOIGTRD ____________________

d. OSUEH-WNGAIRM ____________________

e. DGWIDEN PCREETONI ____________________

f. CEEWLOM OHEM ____________________

LISTENING

1 **Listen to a telephone conversation between two friends. What will Phil's party be like? Tick (✓) the correct picture A, B, C or D.**

A

B

C

D

2 **Phil is writing a note to invite his friend Jake to his birthday party. Listen again and complete the note with the missing information.**

Jake,

I'm having a birthday party on Saturday ____________ 1 at my cousin Paul's house, at 24 ____________ 2 Street. It's going to be a ____________ 3 party, so find something interesting to wear. Please come at around ____________ 4

See you there,

Phil

SPEAKING

1 **Work in pairs. Take turns to be Student A and Student B.**

Student A

Your birthday is in a few days and you are planning to have a party. Invite Student B to your party and answer his/her questions about it.

Student B

Student A is inviting you to his/her birthday party. Accept his/her invitation and ask him/her questions to find out the date, time, place and what you are going to do at the party.

2 **Work in pairs. Imagine that you are organising a party. You are going to invite your friends from school and you want them to have fun. Discuss the ideas below and choose four for your party. Use the expressions given.**

soft drinks

barbecue

board games

music

snacks

magician

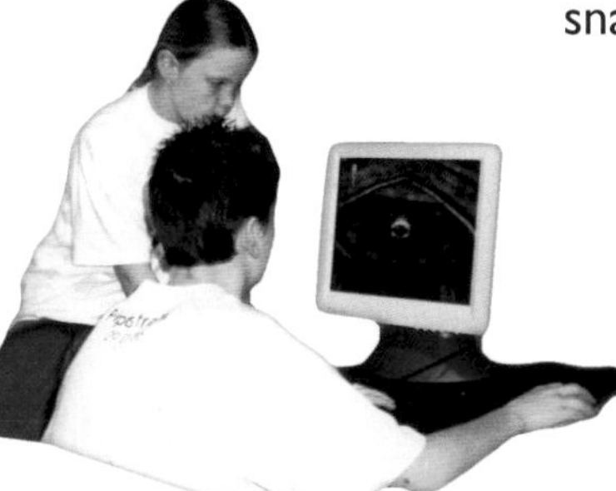
computer games

live band

EXPRESSIONS

I think... is/are a good idea because...
Let's have...
How about having...?
I don't think... is a good idea. It might be...
Shall we make/play/hire...?
Everyone loves... so we must have...
Why don't we buy/get...?
No, ...is/are boring/dangerous.
I would like to... What do you think?

PRE-WRITING

Imagine that you are having a birthday party next week. Write a note to a friend, inviting him/her to your party and giving the necessary details. Look at the note in LISTENING 2.

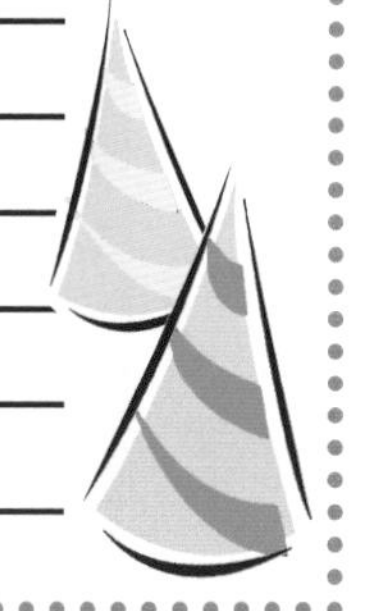

READING

1 **Read the letter below. Six sentences are missing. Complete blanks 1-6 with the sentences A-F.**

38 St Mary's Road
Hatfield
Hertfordshire HT3 25Q
May 9th 2005

Dear Joe,

I was really happy to get your letter. I've got great news, that's why I'm writing back so soon. ______________ (1).

The party is on Sunday 23rd August at lunchtime and it's going to be held in our back garden. ______________ (2). So, we're going to cook steaks and sausages. I know you don't really like meat, but don't worry. ______________ (3). After lunch, it's going to be dancing time! We're going to have my brother's new stereo and I'm thinking of having a dance competition. ______________ (4). You know, the ones we used to listen to together. Finally, whoever wants can even have a swim later in the afternoon. ______________ (5).

I certainly hope you can come. ______________ (6). Don't forget, the party is just a couple of weeks away.

Bye for now,
Bob

A. *So, don't forget to bring your swimwear.*

B. *We're also going to have salads and your favourite - baked potatoes.*

C. *I want to invite you to our house-warming party.*

D. *Please let me know as soon as possible.*

E. *By the way, could you bring some of your CDs?*

F. *It's quite large, with a swimming pool and a barbecue area.*

2 **Read the letter again and look at the picture of the party below. There are four mistakes in the picture. Find them and explain what is wrong.**

WRITING

1 **Read the letter of invitation below. Divide it into three paragraphs and add punctuation (capitals, apostrophes, full stops, commas and question marks).**

crystal road apartments
coral island
April 25th 2005

dear sheila
how are you im here on coral island and im having a wonderful time im writing to invite you to my holiday house next weekend can you make it coral island is a wonderful place and ive made lots of plans for next weekend i know how much you like sailing so on saturday my brother and i are going to hire a boat to go sailing when we get back were going to prepare some food because were going to have a party in the evening all my friends are coming so youll meet them i hope the party is a success anyway on sunday we can go swimming or cycling around the island or do anything else we want well i must go now im sure well have a great time if you come write back and tell me

love
kathy

2 **Below is an incomplete letter of invitation. Read it and complete it using your own ideas. Look at the Remember box on the next page.**

July 16th 2005

Dear Kevin,

How are you? I hope you are fine. I'm writing to invite you to a *Welcome Home* party that we are going to have for my sister, Susan. You are her best friend so I'm sure she'd like to see you.

Susan is coming back from the States in two weeks, on 30th July. Her flight is arriving at noon so all the guests must be here at our house at around half past one. Now let me tell you what we have planned. ______________________________

____

____

____

____

Write back soon,
Kelly

Remember!

- Use the **Future *Going to*** for something that you have planned to do in the future.
- Use **can** to make suggestions.

I'm going to make a chocolate cake for the party.
We **can play** board games after lunch.

3 Imagine that it is the end of the school year and that you are planning to have a party. Answer the questions below in note form.

When are you having the party? ____________________

Where is it going to take place? ____________________

Who are you going to invite? ____________________

What are you going to do? 1 ____________________

2 ____________________

3 ____________________

4 ____________________

Remember!

When you are writing a letter of invitation, you should write three paragraphs.

- In the first paragraph, use set phrases to invite the person you are writing to.
  e.g. *How are you? I'm writing to invite you to ...*
  I've got some news for you. I'm having a party and I would like to invite you.
- In the second paragraph, give information about the date, time, place, activities, etc. You can answer the questions in WRITING 3.
- In the third paragraph, use set phrases to end your letter.
  e.g. *I hope you can come. I can't wait to see you!*
  I'm looking forward to seeing you.

PROJECT

Turn to page 91 and write a letter to a friend, inviting him/her to a party to celebrate the end of the school year. Use the notes you made in WRITING 3.

A world of adventure

WARM-UP

1 Look at the grid below and find fourteen verbs related to adventure.

D	A	E	I	M	P	S	A	T	T	A	C	K	D	H
I	X	D	J	H	E	K	O	P	T	R	H	L	H	I
S	H	O	U	T	V	X	F	B	Y	S	A	V	E	D
C	E	X	M	D	G	H	P	C	E	C	S	V	U	E
O	Z	A	P	E	F	O	L	L	O	W	E	G	E	I
V	J	M	R	Z	A	C	R	I	O	A	L	N	A	L
E	R	F	S	C	R	E	A	M	M	R	E	W	Q	N
R	C	G	K	O	H	V	B	B	W	N	E	J	F	B

2 Below is the beginning of a story. Work in groups and take turns to continue the story. Each of you should make a sentence using one of the words in the box. Continue until the story is finished.

suddenly	immediately	then	luckily	unfortunately	later	finally

Terry and Cindy were driving their jeep through the Sahara Desert. It was noon and the sun was burning. The nearest oasis was two hundred kilometres away ...

Remember !

- When you are telling a story, use **adverbs** like the ones shown above.

LISTENING

1 **Listen to a student telling a fairy tale in class. What did Jack get at the end of each day for his work? In each of the bubbles below draw a picture and/or write the answer, as in the example.**

2 **Listen to the recording again and read the sentences below. Write T for True or F for False in the boxes.**

a. Stephen's mother told him the fairy tale. ☐

b. Jack put the money in his pocket. ☐

c. Jack spilt the milk on his way home. ☐

d. Jack tied a string to an animal and pulled it along. ☐

e. Jack carried an animal on his shoulders. ☐

f. The story has a happy ending. ☐

SPEAKING

1 **Work in pairs. Student A, look at the comic strip below and Student B, look at the comic strip on the next page. Don't look at each other's comic strips. Student A, narrate the story shown in your comic strip. Use the vocabulary given. Student B, find a possible ending for Student A's story. Then, narrate the story shown in your comic strip using the vocabulary given. Student A find a possible ending for it.**

VOCABULARY

boy scouts	forest	spread	put up flag	run towards
picnic	river	tablecloth	bull nearby	shout

VOCABULARY

shipwreck	hold on to	island	beach	straw skirts
survive	piece of wood	lie	natives	painted faces

2 **Work in groups of three. Below are three boxes of words, one for each group. Take turns to make up a short story based on the words you have and narrate it to your group.**

Meg and Jeff	tiger
safari	chase
jungle	Tarzan
wild animals	save

Ann	follow directions
cave	treasure
explore	museum
map	reward

Steve	hit rock
river	turn over
canoe	fall in
lose paddles	swim shore

PRE-WRITING

Look at the comic strip below and write what happened. Use the vocabulary given.

____

____

____

____

____

VOCABULARY

toy shop	point at	floor	slip	security guard
cash desk	cashier	robber	fall down	pick up
gun	throw	step on	drop	arrest

READING

1 **Read the first paragraph of the story below. What information does this paragraph give? Then, read the rest of the story and put the pictures A-F below in the correct order by writing the numbers 1-6 in the boxes.**

It was a very hot summer morning, but inside the Pyramid it was quite cool. Tom and his classmates had just entered the Pyramid and were very curious to see what it was like.

The guide took them to the Queen's Chamber first. There, she showed them a passage which led to a small room. 'No one is allowed to go into that room, because it was recently discovered', she said. As she continued talking, Tom looked towards the passage. Two of his friends, Jason and Peter, saw him and warned him, 'Don't get into trouble, Tom!' However, he didn't listen to them. As soon as no one was looking, he went up the dark passage, opened the door and walked in. Suddenly, the door shut behind him. The room was completely dark, but luckily Tom had brought a torch with him. When he turned it on, he saw two white faces in front of him. 'Oh, no! Mummies!' he screamed and ran to the door. He quickly opened it and went down the passage to the Queen's Chamber as fast as he could.

As soon as Tom had disappeared, Jason and Peter took the pieces of white cloth off their faces and walked slowly down the passage. They couldn't stop laughing. 'That will teach him a lesson,' said Jason.

2 **Read the story again and choose the best answer a, b or c.**

1 Why did Jason and Peter say "Don't get into trouble, Tom!"?
 a. because they knew that Tom was thinking of doing something bad
 b. because Tom had got into trouble earlier that day
 c. because Tom hadn't heard what the guide had said

2 What did Tom do when the door closed behind him?
 a. He panicked and screamed.
 b. He waited quietly in the dark.
 c. He turned his torch on.

3 Why were Jason and Peter laughing?
 a. because they had got Tom into trouble
 b. because they liked telling jokes
 c. because they had played a trick on Tom

WRITING

1 **Read the story below and complete the sentences with the Past Simple, the Past Progressive or the Past Perfect of the verbs in brackets. Look at the Remember box.**

One day Joe and Simon (**1**)________________ (set out) to explore the northern part of the forest. They (**2**)________________ (not be) to that part of the forest before.

The boys (**3**)________________ (decide) to climb up to Crystal Falls first. While they (**4**)________________ (climb), they could hear the sound of falling water. When they (**5**)________________ (reach) the top, they (**6**)________________ (see) the amazing waterfall. It was the most beautiful thing they (**7**)________________ (see) on their trip so far. After they (**8**)________________ (rest) there for a while, they (**9**)________________ (take) out some sandwiches that they (**10**)________________ (bring) with them in their backpacks. As they (**11**)________________ (eat), Joe (**12**)________________ (discover) a path through some very tall trees. So, they (**13**)________________ (follow) the path and before long they (**14**)________________ (arrive) in front of a gate. Behind it was a beautiful castle. The boys got excited and (**15**)________________ (spend) the rest of the day there. They (**16**)________________ (love) the idea of exploring a castle.

When they finally (**17**)________________ (decide) to go home, it (**18**)________________ (get) dark. They (**19**)________________ (not care) though, because they (**20**)________________ (have) a wonderful time.

Remember !

- When you are writing a story, use the **Past Simple** and the **Past Progressive** (see page 23). You can also use the **Past Perfect Simple** for something that happened before a past event.

Margaret **had tried** to put out the fire herself before she **called** the fire brigade.

2 Read the story below and circle the correct linking words/phrases.

Debbie got up early on that sunny Saturday morning. She had arranged to go on a picnic to Green Park with her friends and she was very excited about it.

As soon as / While she was ready, she got on her bike and headed for the park which was on the other side of the town. Suddenly, **as / after** she was riding through the town centre, she heard sirens. The sound of the sirens was getting closer and closer, **but / so** Debbie looked behind her to see what was happening. **As a result / Before**, she lost control of her bike and fell off. Her bike ended up in the middle of the road. Luckily, Debbie wasn't hurt, **but / when** a car ran over her bike. **Soon / After** the car had stopped, two men got out and started running. **Just then / For this reason**, a police car stopped next to the same car and three police officers got out and started chasing the two men. One of the officers shouted, "Stop the thieves!"

Some time **later / finally** a police officer offered Debbie a reward. She was the heroine of the day **because / however**, in a way, she had helped them catch the thieves.

- Use **linking words/phrases** when you are writing. Look at the ones shown below.

when	after a while	later	because
while	before	finally	so
as	before long	just then	as a result
as soon as	soon	however	for this reason
after	then	but	

3 **Below is the first and last paragraph of a story. Look at the pictures and use the notes given to complete the main part of the story.**

One Sunday morning Arthur and Christine decided to go for a walk in the forest. It was the beginning of spring and it was quite warm and sunny.

____

____

____

____

____

____

____

____

____

____

The children ran for help and soon a helicopter arrived to take the man to hospital. He was the owner of the parrot. He asked the children to look after the parrot while he was in hospital. Arthur and Christine were delighted.

- As / they / walk / through forest / see / large parrot
- It / say / "Follow me! Follow me!"
- Children / get excited / decide / follow parrot

- After a while / they / come to / narrow bridge
- Children / be frightened / but / continue

- When / they / cross bridge / parrot / land on / tree / near cliff
- Children / stop
- Just then / they / hear / someone / calling for help

- They / look around / see / man / edge of cliff
- He / lie down / because / fall / break leg

Remember!

When you are writing a story, you should write three paragraphs.

- In the first paragraph, mention the main characters and describe the setting (*place, weather, time*).
- In the second paragraph, describe what happened.
- In the third paragraph, describe what happened in the end.

Don't forget to use adverbs and linking words/phrases in your story.

PROJECT

The pictures below show a story, but the ending is missing. Turn to page 93 and write the story, as well as a possible ending. You can use the vocabulary given. In the space provided, draw a picture which shows what happened in the end.

VOCABULARY

evening	carriage
funfair	press button
closed	round and round
jump over fence	top of wheel
ferris wheel	scream

Here's my advice

WARM-UP

1 The following teenagers have got problems and have written to the problem page of a teenage magazine asking for advice. Read their problems and the advice *Helpful Harriet* has given them. Then match each problem with the correct piece of advice. Write the teenagers' names in the spaces 1-6 below.

I play in a basketball team and have to train a lot so I haven't got enough time to study. What should I do?

My next-door neighbours play loud music every night and I can't sleep. What should I do?

I'm a very shy person and my problem is that I can't make friends easily. What should I do?

I like borrowing my sister's clothes but she doesn't agree because she's afraid I'll ruin them. So, we always argue. What should I do?

My parents are always complaining that I don't help them around the house, but the truth is that I haven't got enough time. I also think it's very boring! What should I do?

I want to buy a CD player, but my parents won't give me the money because they have just bought me a computer. What should I do?

PROBLEM PAGE

Here's my advice by Helpful Harriet

1 Dear ____________ ,
You should try talking to them. If that doesn't work, call the police.

2 Dear ____________ ,
Most people find household chores boring, but someone has to do them! You should a least find some time to tidy your bedroom once a week.

3 Dear ____________ ,
Don't you think you're asking for too much? Perhaps you should save up your pocket money and buy it yourself.

4 Dear ____________ ,
You shouldn't be afraid to talk to people. Perhaps you should take up a team sport or join a club.

5 Dear ____________ ,
You should organise your time more carefully. Try doing some homework at the weekend.

6 Dear ____________ ,
You shouldn't borrow your sister's things all the time. When you do, ask her first and make sure you look after them.

LISTENING

1 Listen to a conversation between two friends. Circle a, b or c.

Why did Ian get angry at John?

a. because John wanted to play Ian's computer game, too

b. because John damaged Ian's keyboard

c. because John made Ian lose the game

2 Listen to a conversation between Ian and another friend of his, Mark. What advice does Mark give Ian? Read the sentences below and tick (✓) the correct boxes.

a. You shouldn't be rude to your friends. ☐

b. You shouldn't play computer games when you are with your friends. ☐

c. You should invite John to play computer games with you. ☐

d. You should spend more time with your friends. ☐

e. You should tell John that you are sorry. ☐

f. You should wait until John apologises first. ☐

SPEAKING

1 Work in pairs. Think of a problem you have had recently and take turns to interview each other. Use the questions below.

1 Who/What did your problem involve?
parents? brother(s)/sister(s)?
friends? school?

2 What was wrong?

3 Who did you ask for advice?

4 What advice did you get? Did it help you?

2 **Work in groups of three. Imagine that you have got one of the problems A, B or C below. Then take turns to tell your problem to the other two students in your group. They should give you some advice, using the expressions in the Remember box.**

A

My sister and I share the same bedroom and she always throws her clothes everywhere. I have told her that I don't like the mess, but she doesn't care. We always argue. What should I do?

B

Yesterday evening, as I was going past my school, I saw two boys breaking into the school. Today our headteacher asked us if we knew anything about the break-in. I know that I must tell him what I saw, but I don't want to get into trouble. What should I do?

C

Every Saturday and Sunday my friends and I go to fast food restaurants. We eat and have a good time, but I have put on weight. I have explained my problem to my friends, but they don't want to go anywhere else. What should I do?

Remember !

When you are giving advice, you can use:

- You **should (not)** ...
- Why don't you ...?
- How/What about ...?
- It's (not) a good idea to ...

I think you **should apologise** to your friend.

You **shouldn't go** out by yourself at night.

PRE-WRITING

Choose one of the problems A, B or C in SPEAKING 2 and write a few sentences giving advice.

I think you should ...

READING

1 **Francis has got some problems and has written the letter below to her sister Mary. Read the letter. What advice can you give Francis?**

6 St Helen's Way
Ipswich
Suffolk IP5 3W5
February 22th 2005

Dear Mary,

I hope you are well because I'm not. I'm having problems with mum and dad and I want to leave home. I really need your advice.

Mum and dad think I'm a child. Last night I went out and came back at midnight. They were still up waiting for me and we had a fight. They think I stay out too late, but my friends stay out even later than I do! It's not fair! And this is not the only problem. Mum still wants to buy all my clothes for me. Of course, I don't like what she buys because she never gets me anything that's in fashion. What should I do, Mary? Can I come and live with you?

Please write back soon.

Yours,
Francis

Now read Mary's letter to Francis. Is Mary's advice the same as the advice you suggested?

23 Park Avenue
Epsom
Surrey KT51 3LR
March 5th 2005

Dear Francis,

I got your letter today and I'm writing back immediately. I'm sorry to hear that you're so upset.

I don't think that it's a good idea to leave home and come and live with me. You must solve your problems, not run away from them! You're right, mum and dad shouldn't treat you like a child, but don't forget - you're only fifteen and they worry about you. Why don't you explain to them how you feel? Tell them that you're growing up and need more freedom. But every time you go out, you should tell them where you're going and who you are going to be with. Then they won't worry so much. You should also tell mum that you want to go shopping with her. I'm sure she will understand. If you show her the kind of clothes you like, she'll buy you what you want. Take my advice and you'll see that things aren't as bad as you think.

I really hope everything goes well. Write back and let me know how it goes.

Love,
Mary

2 **Read the two letters again and complete the table below.**

Francis' problems	Mary's advice
1.	
2.	
3.	

WRITING

1 **Read the problem below which appeared in a teenage magazine and give some advice. Match the phrases in boxes A and B and then write full sentences. Begin with *I think you should/shouldn't ...* or *Perhaps you should/shouldn't ...***

PROBLEM PAGE

My best friend has been depressed lately and I'm worried about him. A couple of months ago he was fine. He enjoyed going out and we had lots of laughs together. Now, he just wants to stay at home alone. He's also very moody. What should I do to help him?

Anxious, 17

A

- don't worry too much about him
- organise a small party
- visit him more often
- take him to the cinema to watch a comedy
- don't get angry with him

B

- because that will make him feel better
- if he doesn't talk to you
- because many teenagers go through similar phases
- because then he will know that you care
- so he can meet new people and have fun

e.g. I think you shouldn't worry too much about him because many teenagers go through similar phases.

a. ______________________________

b. ______________________________

c. ______________________________

d. ______________________________

2 Imagine that a friend of yours has sent you the letter below. What advice can you give him/her? Make notes in the space below the letter.

Dear __________,

How are you? I hope you feel better than I do. I'm writing to tell you my problem and to see if you can give me some advice.

It's the second week of the summer holidays and I'm terribly bored already! I can't find anything to do, so I spend my time at home watching DVDs. All my friends have gone away on holiday, like you. However, my parents won't have time off work until next month, so I'm stuck here! The only people in my neighbourhood are my new neighbours. I feel miserable! Boredom is driving me crazy! What should I do?

Let me know what you think as soon as possible.

Your friend,

____

Advice:
1 ______________________________
2 ______________________________
3 ______________________________
4 ______________________________

Remember!

When you are writing a letter giving advice, you should write three paragraphs.

- In the first paragraph, use set phrases to begin your letter.
  e.g. *How are you? I'm writing to give you some advice.*
  I hope you're doing better.
  I'm sorry to hear that you've got problems.
  I've given your problem a lot of thought.
- In the second paragraph, give your advice.
- In the third paragraph, use a set phrase to end your letter.
  e.g. *Well, that's what I think you should do.*
  I hope my advice will help you.
  Well, that's all the advice I can give you.
  I hope everything goes well.

PROJECT

Read the letter in WRITING 2 again. Then turn to page 95 and write a letter to your friend, giving him/her advice on his/her problem. Use the notes you made in WRITING 2.

Project pages

PROJECT 1

About myself

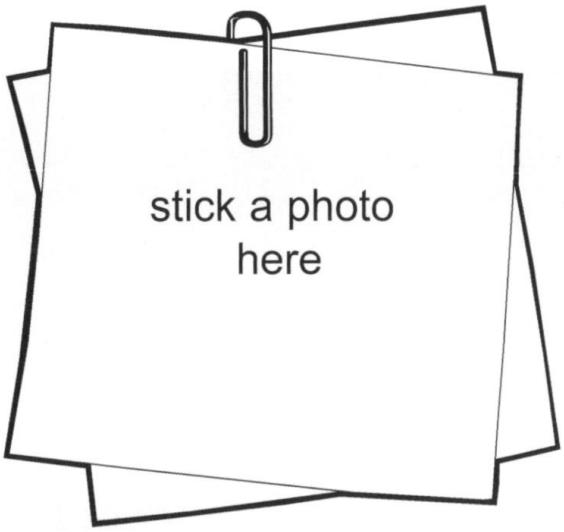

stick a photo here

Dear ______________,

Hello! I'm very happy we will be penfriends. Let me tell you about myself.

Well, I'm looking forward to hearing from you. Please write soon.

Bye for now,

PROJECT 2

My town

PROJECT 3

This is what happened

PROJECT 4

My holidays

PROJECT 5

Superstars!

PROJECT 6

In the future

PROJECT 7

A film I saw

PROJECT 8

Would you like to come?

A world of adventure

Here's my advice